Photography

colorblind

Being colorblind gives an advantage when composing black & white… less confusion.
This special collection selected from thousands of captures. All images were framed
in the camera and presented without edits, genuine as seen through the lens.
Panchromatic conversion applied by unique proprietary process.
Original fine art and custom work available.

info@ BEACHNOISE.com

Joseph Fleming

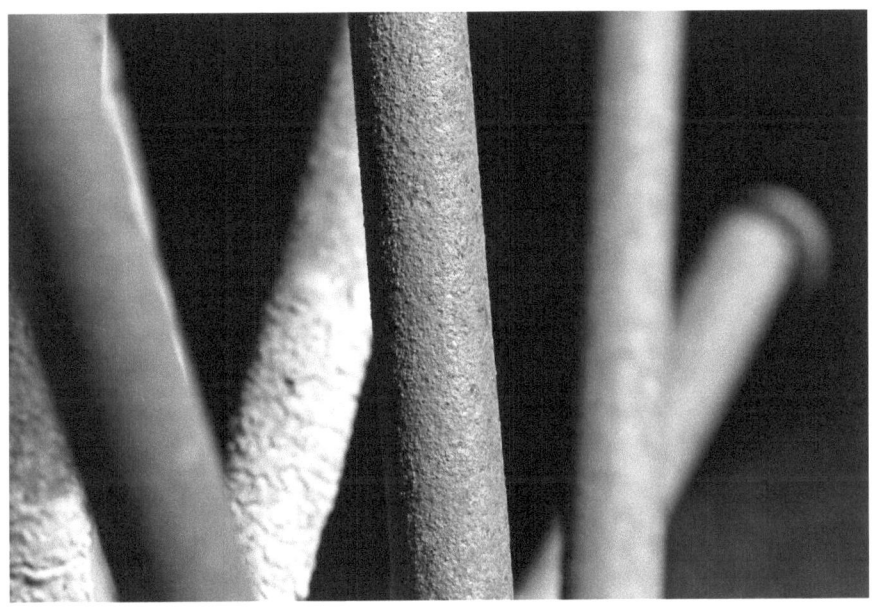

0780

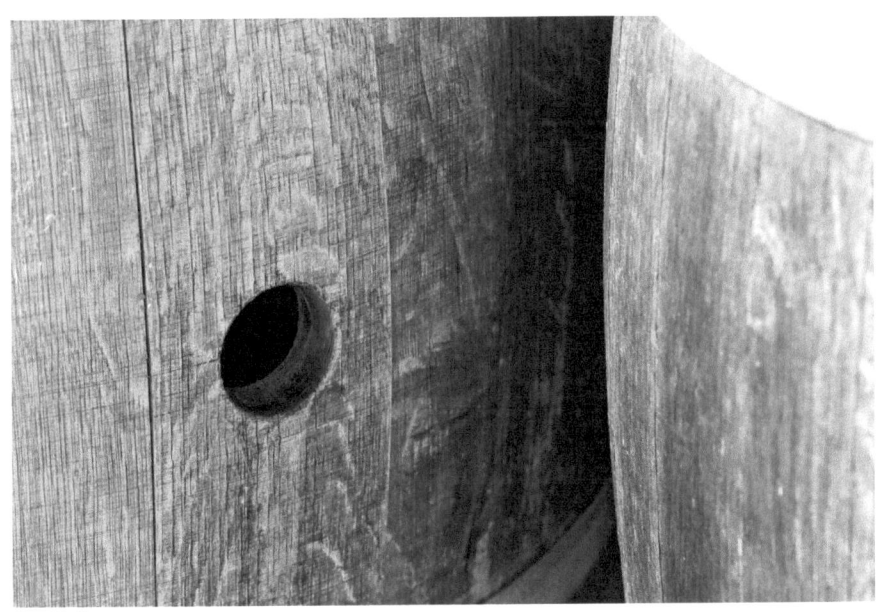

0826

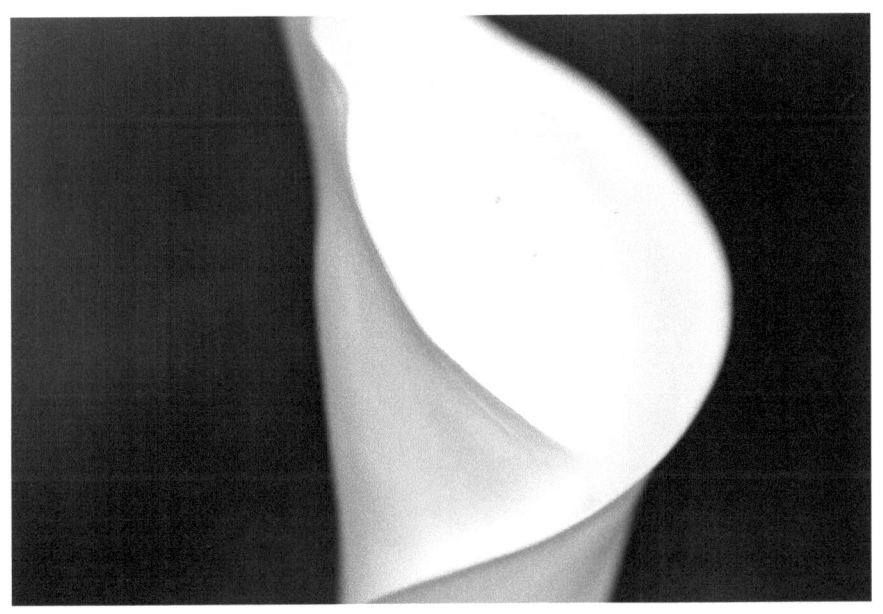

0920

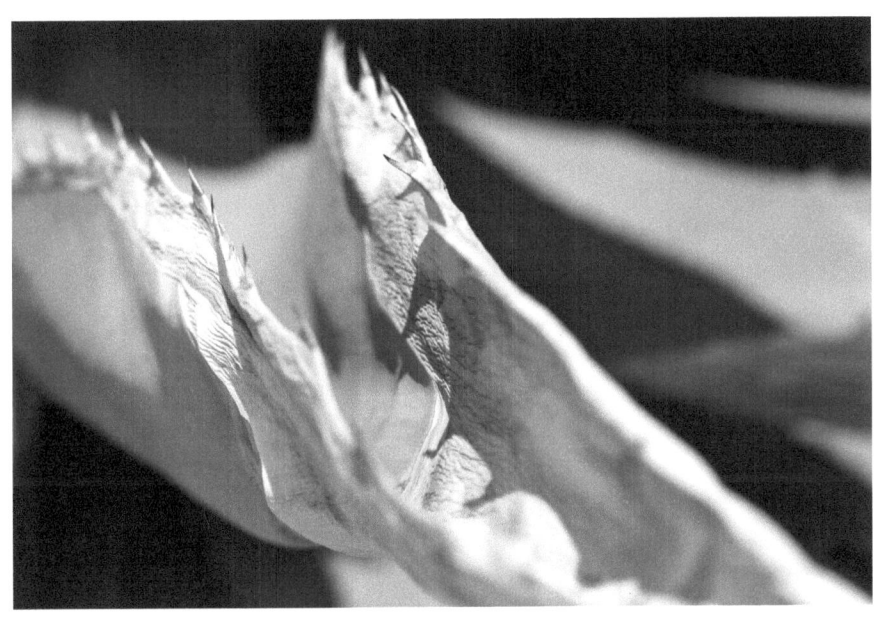

1581

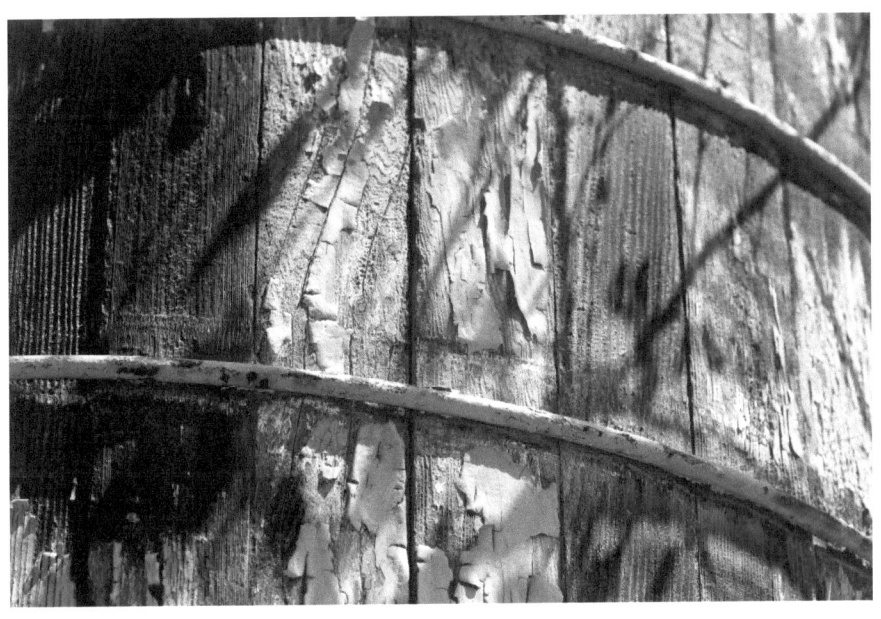

1608

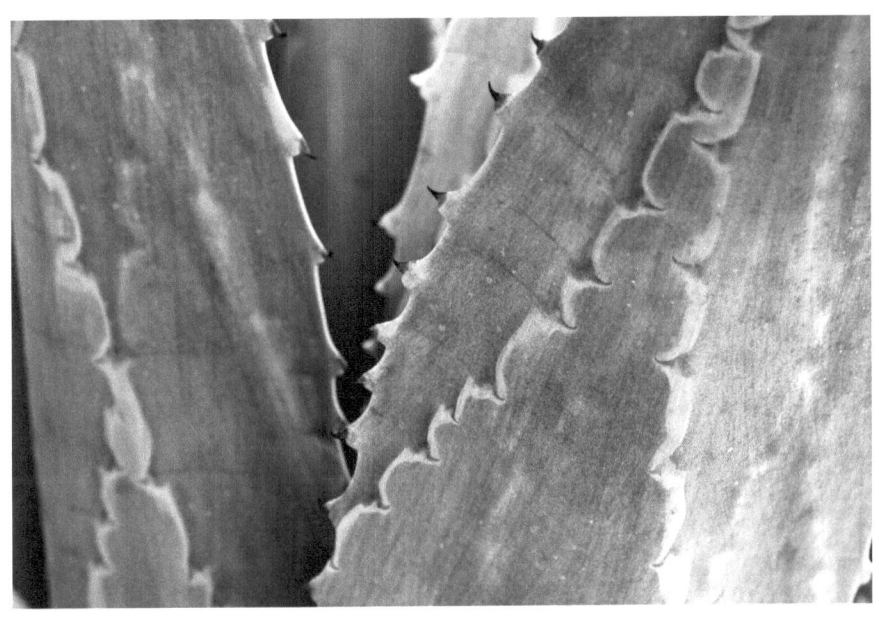

1976

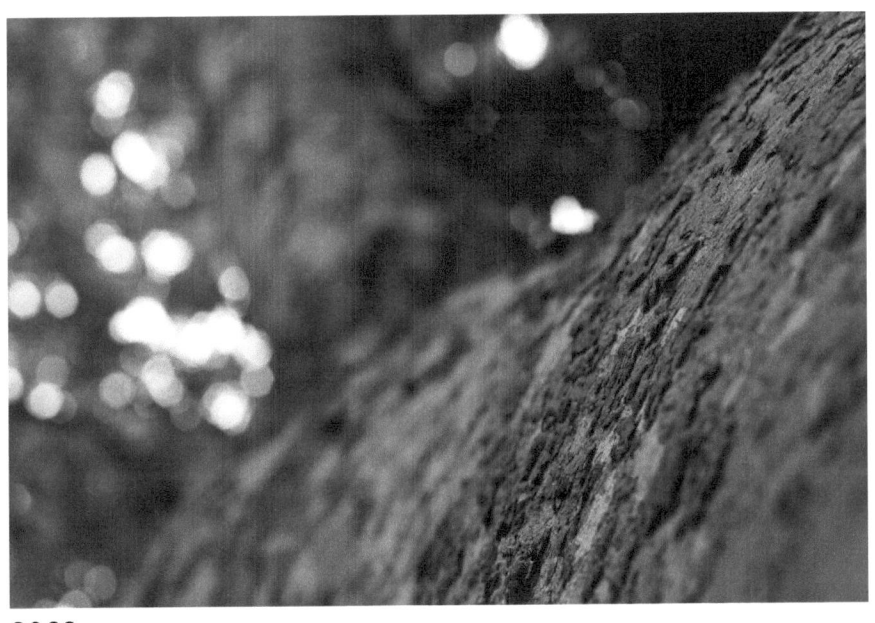

2068

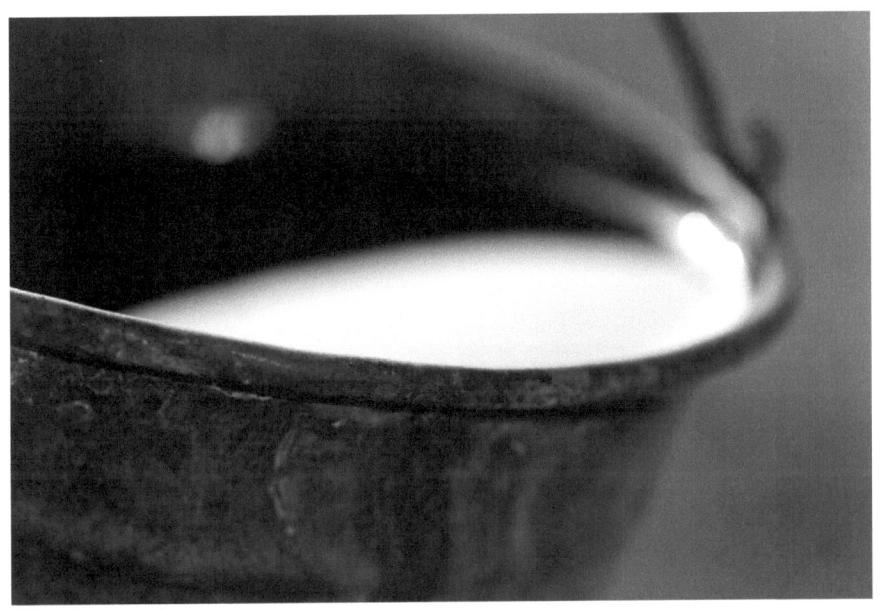

2180

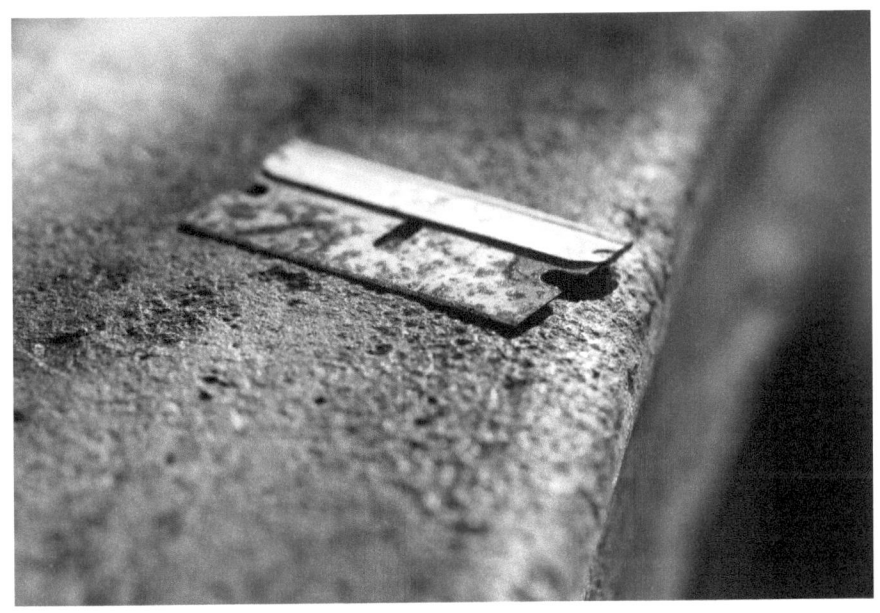

2467

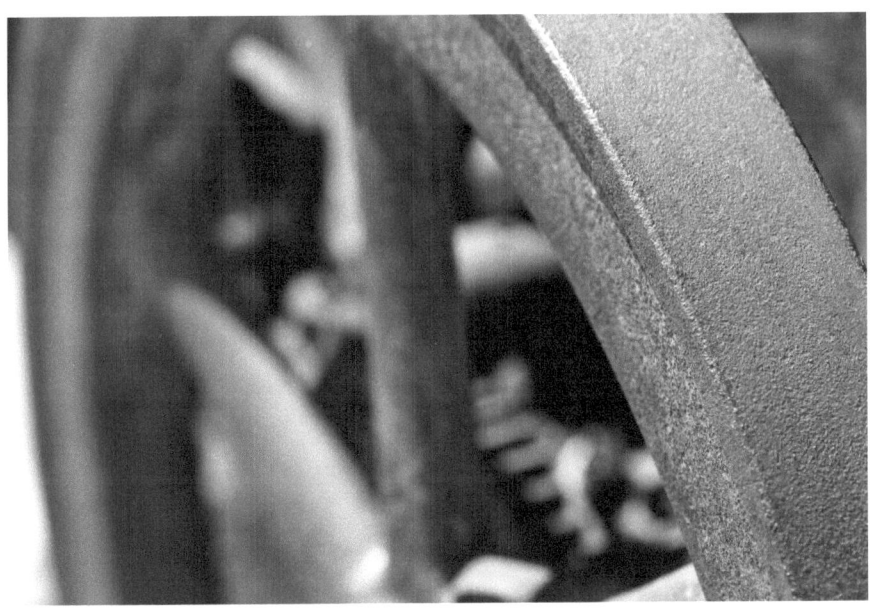

2962

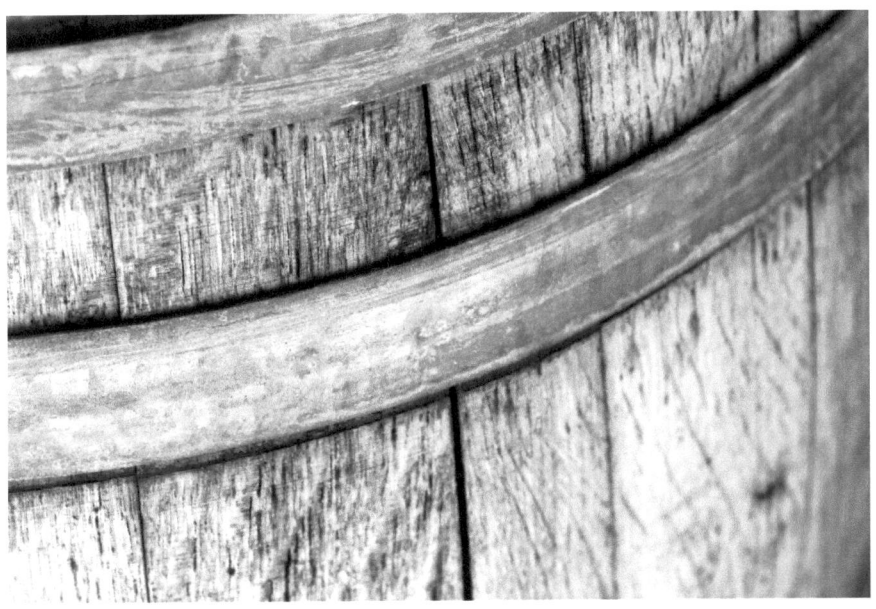

3151

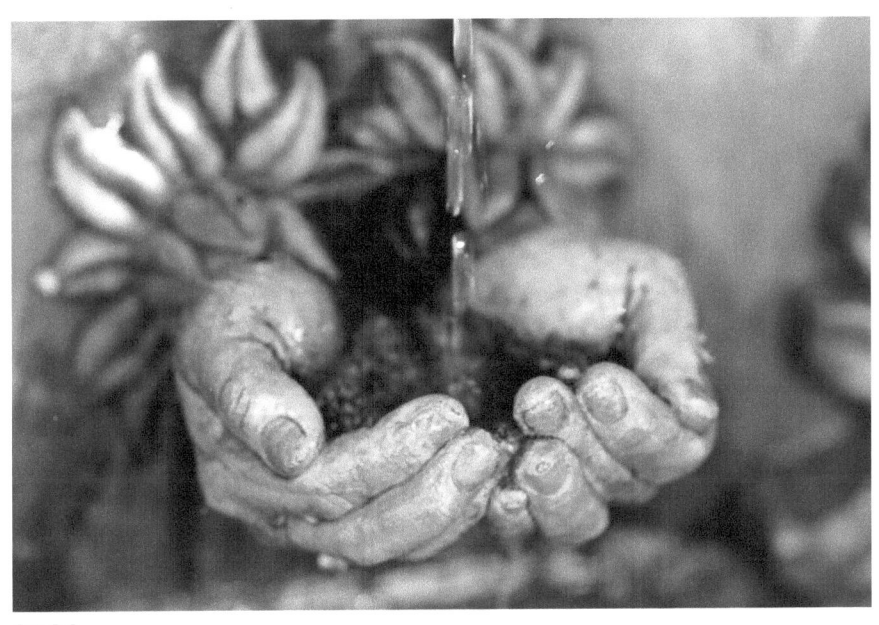

3720

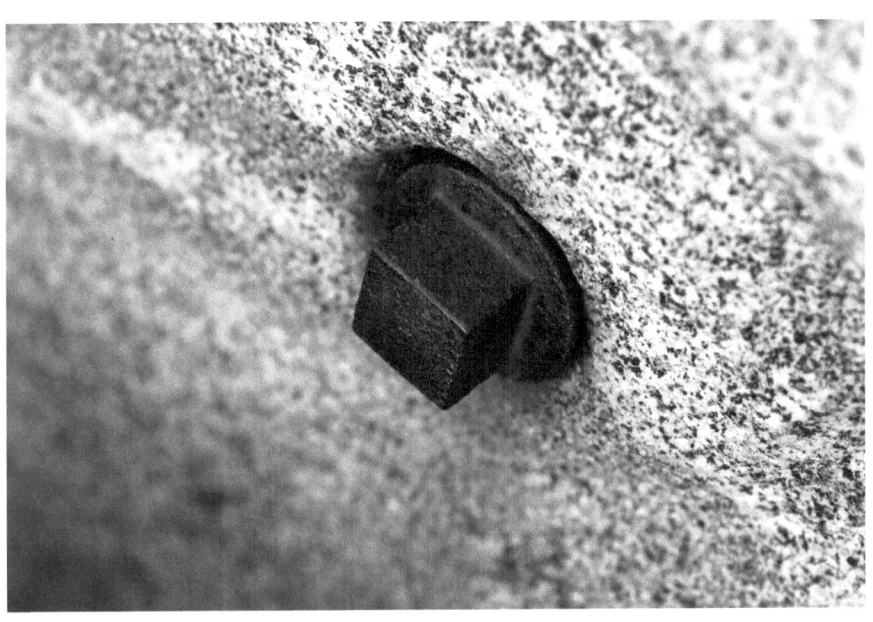

4035

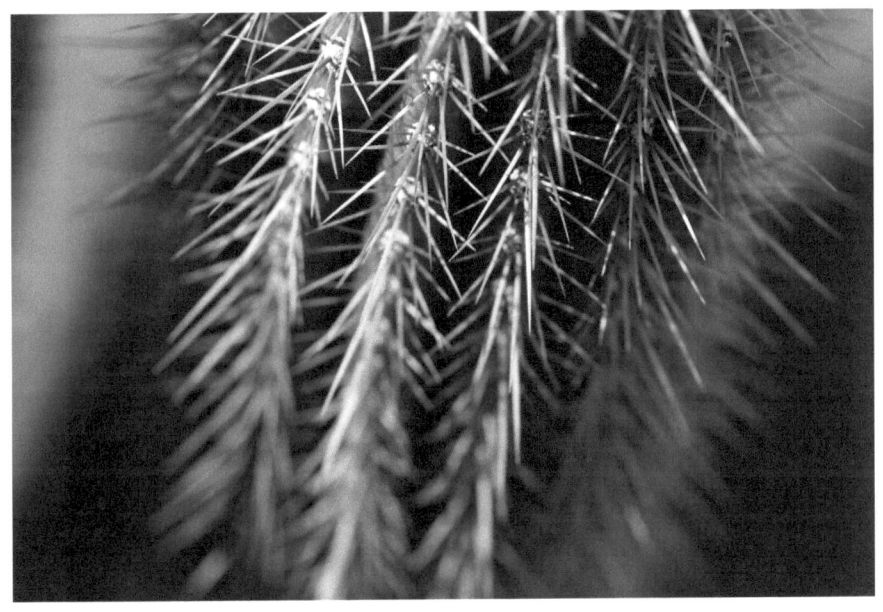

4070

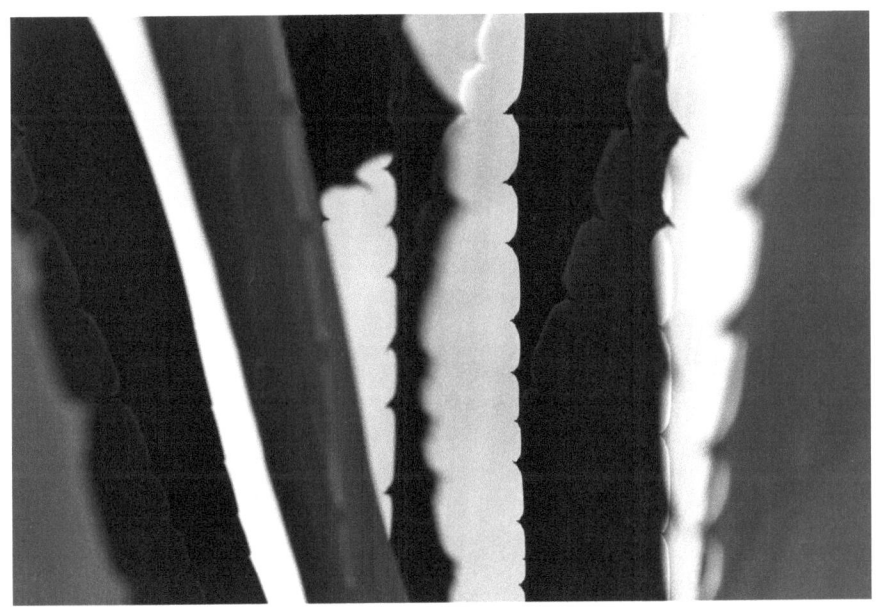

4099

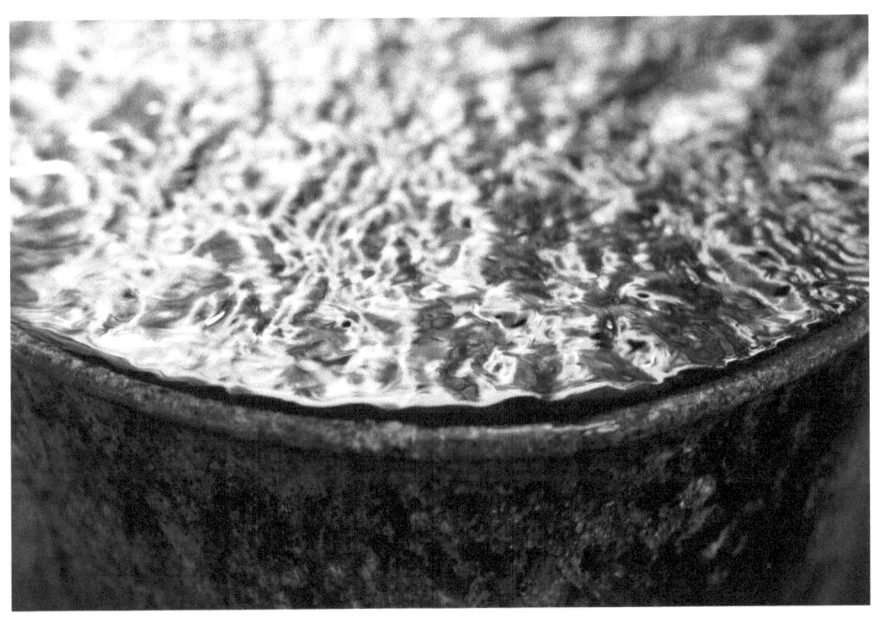

4533

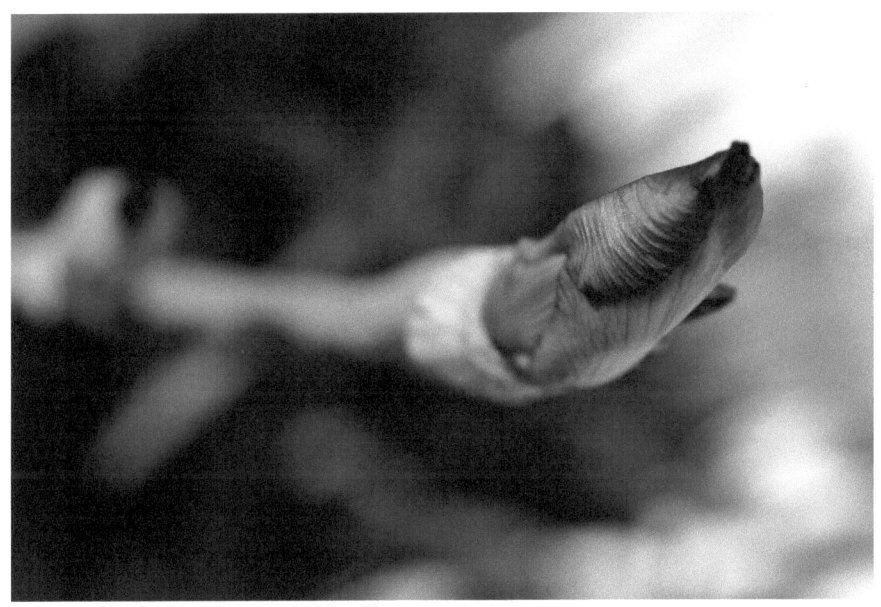

5492

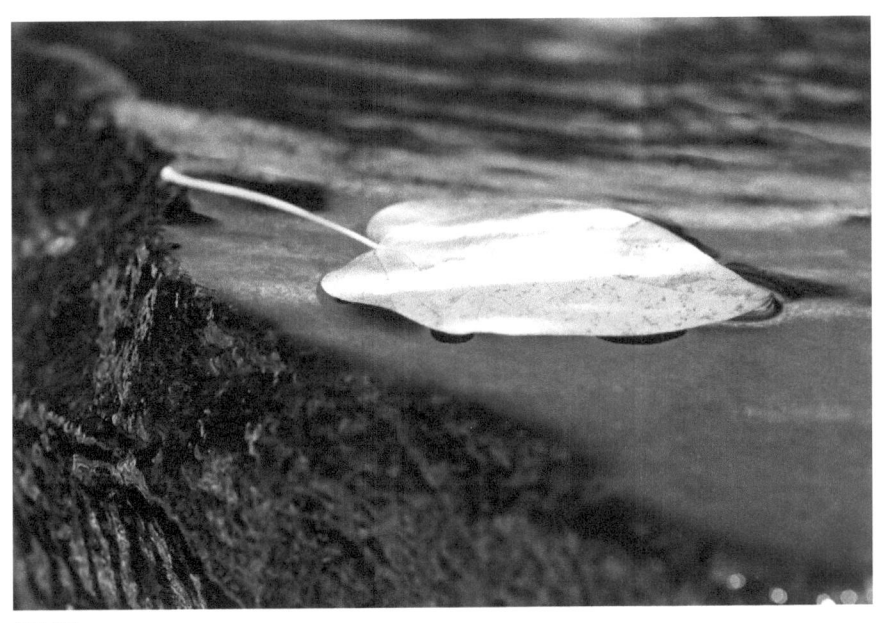

5750

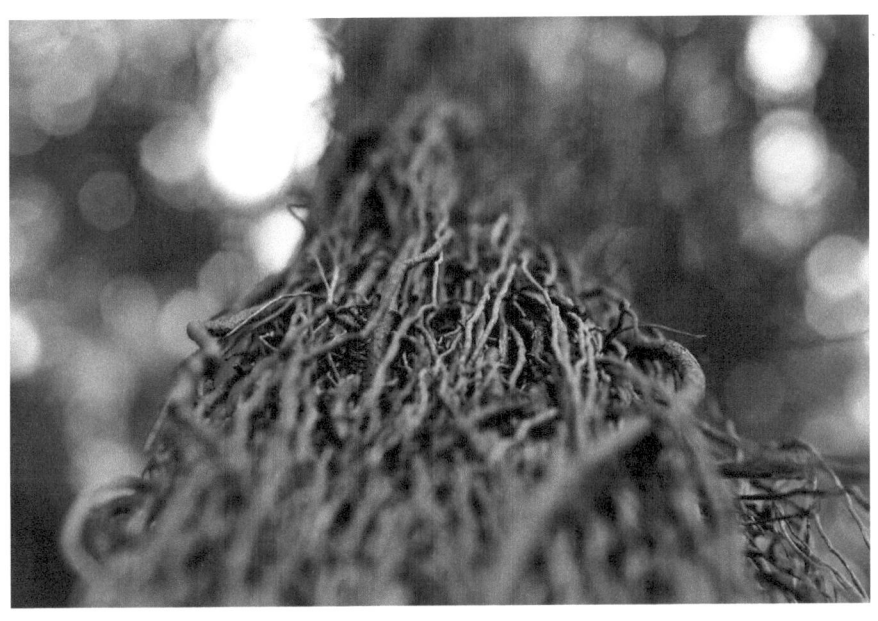

5811

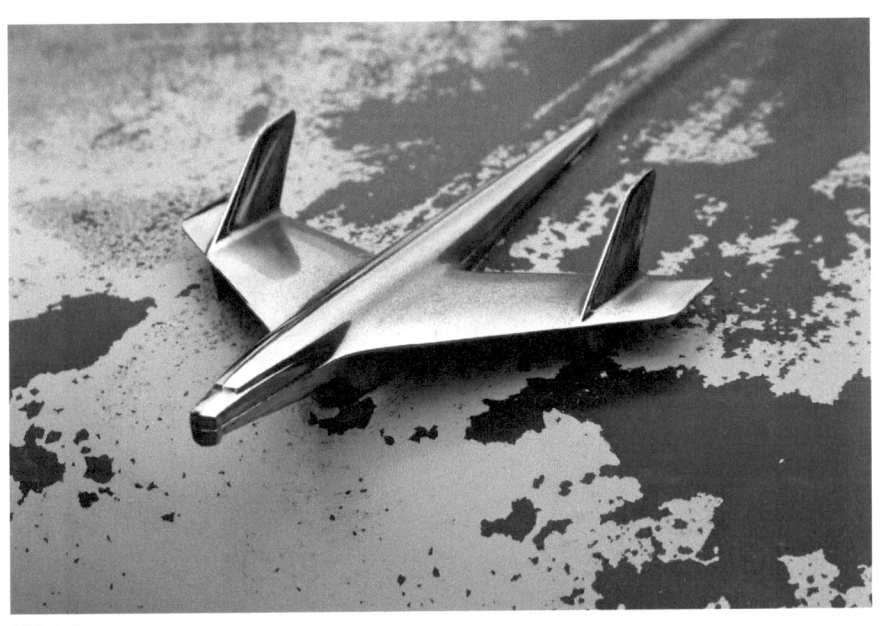

5846

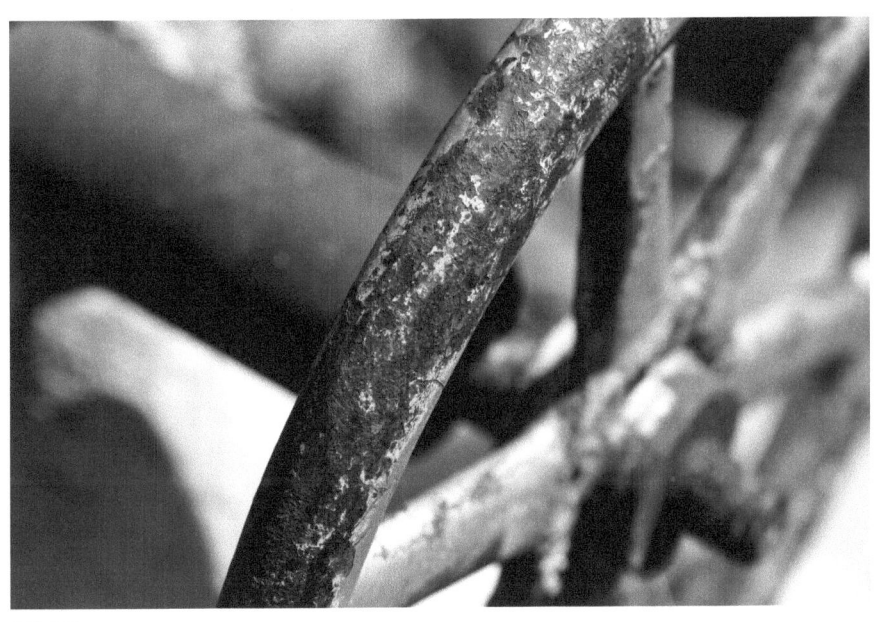

6095

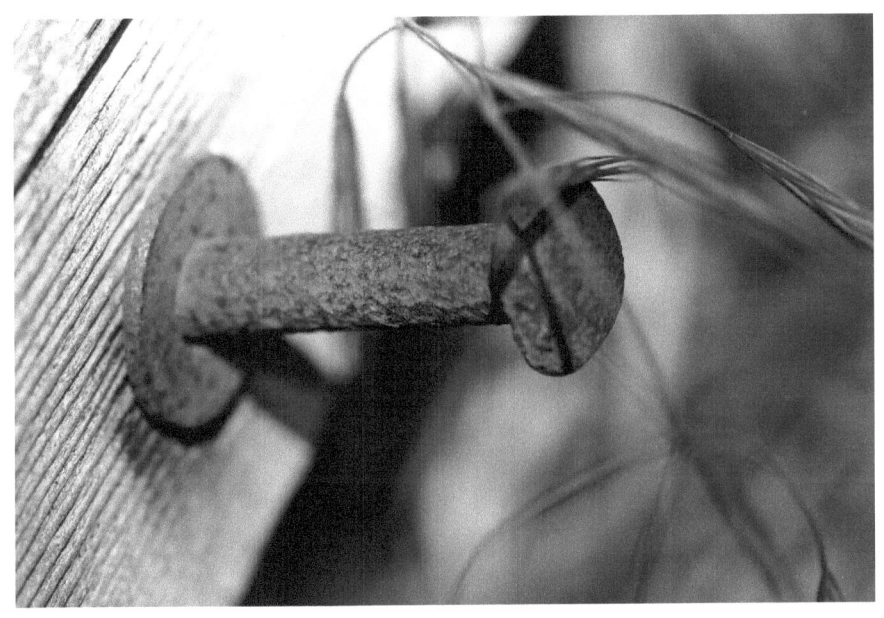

7182

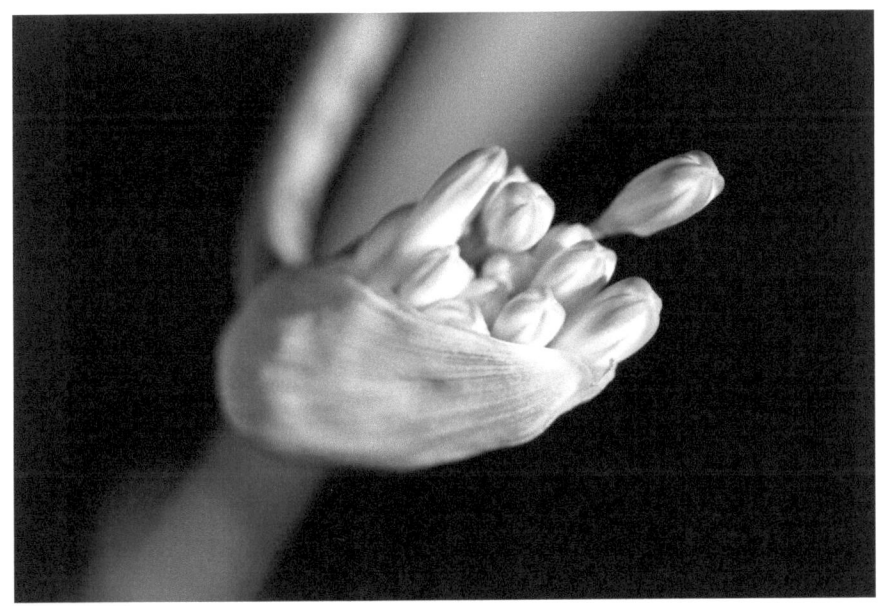

8407

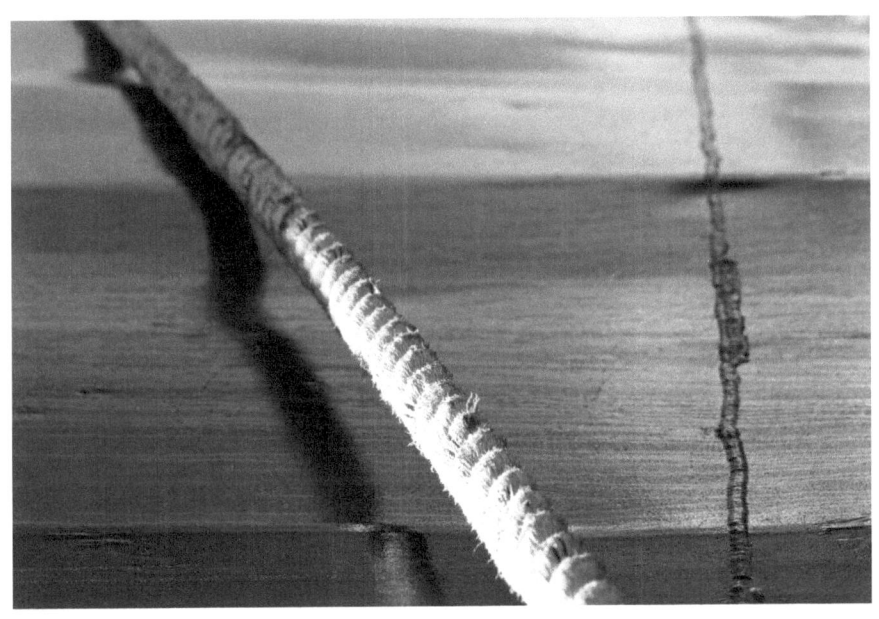

8470

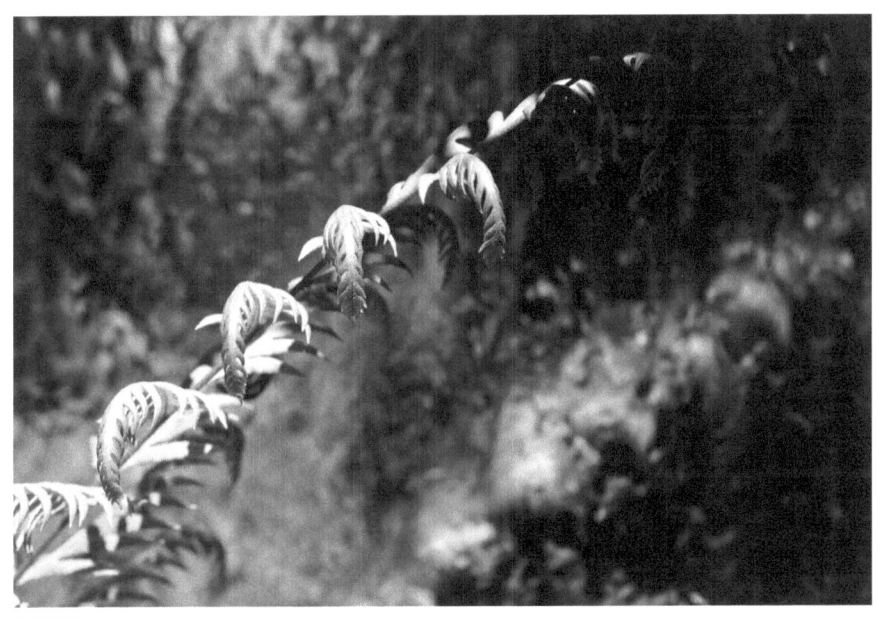

8889

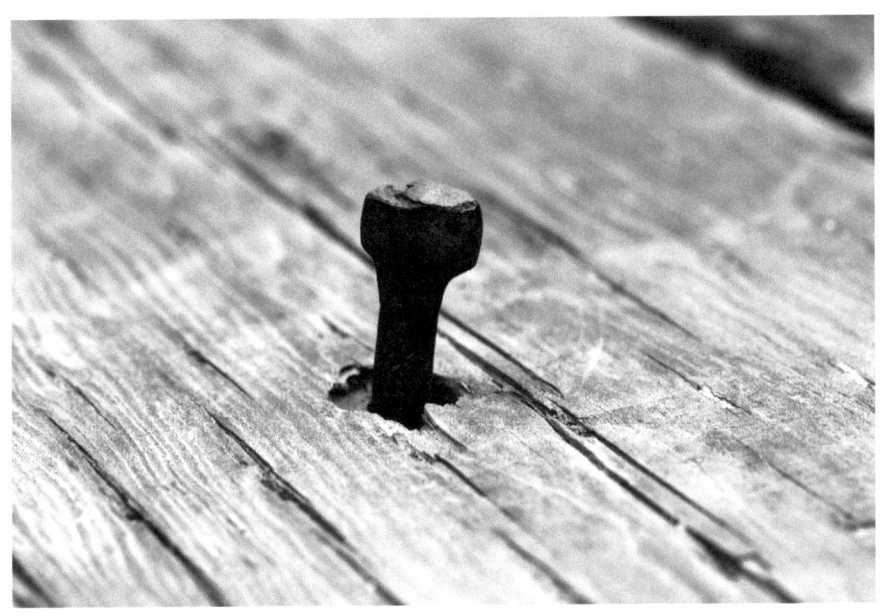

9024

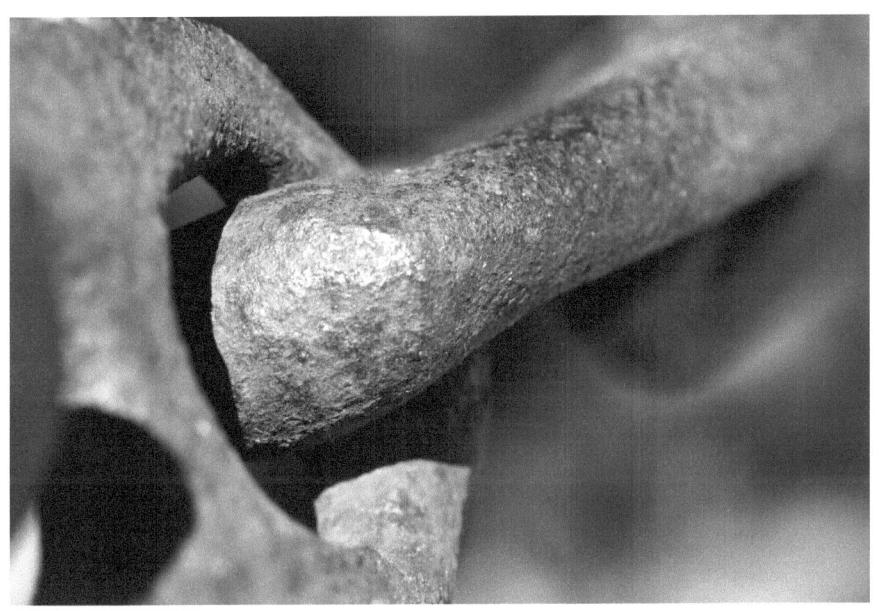

9353

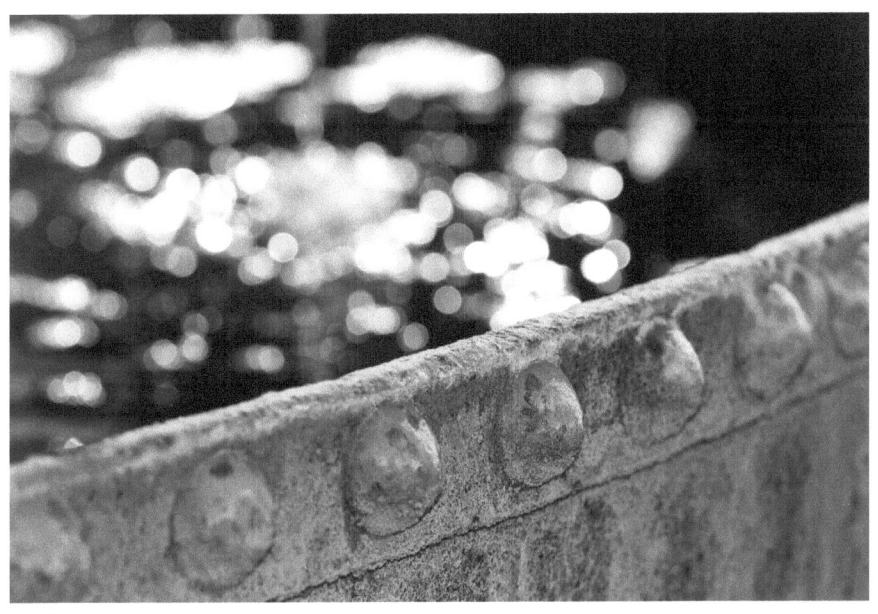

9430

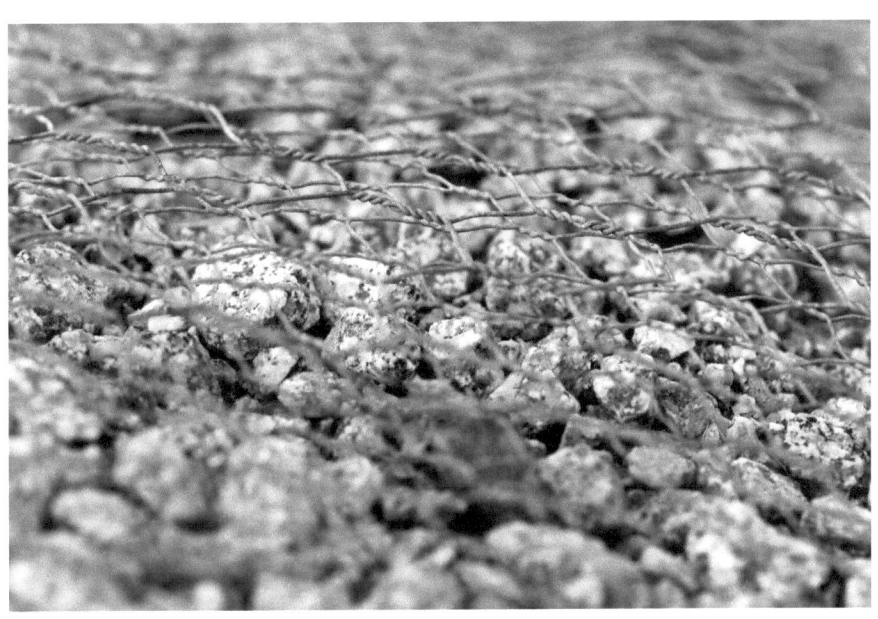

9970

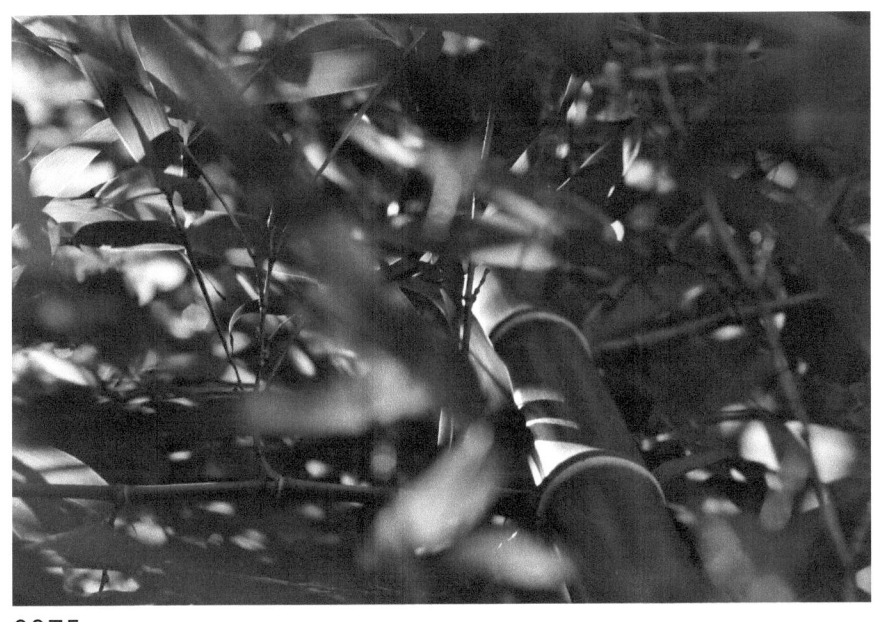

9975

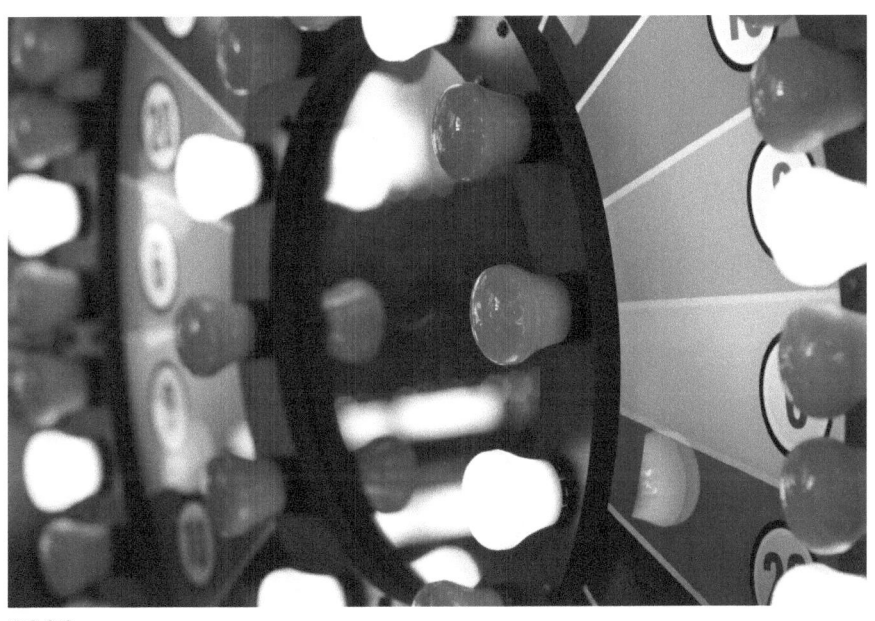

9980

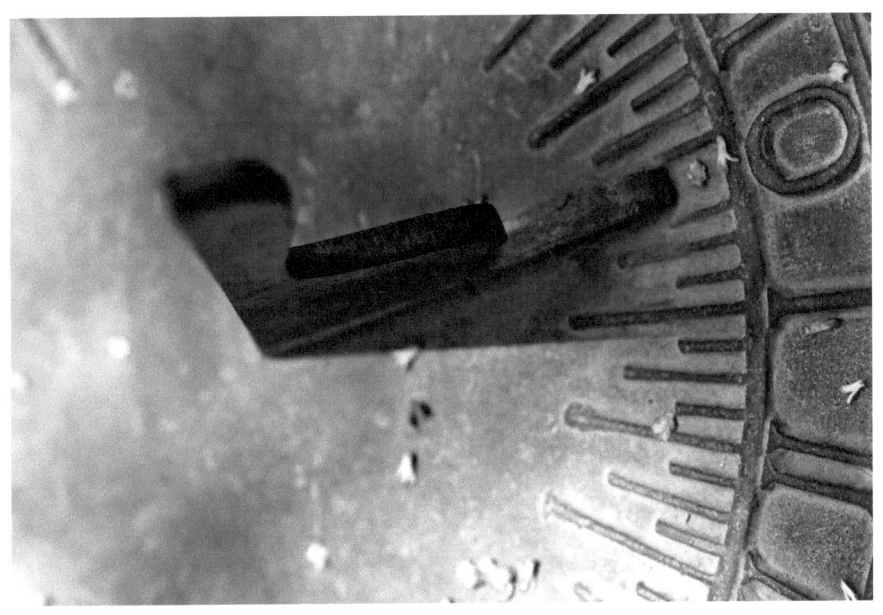

10002

www.ingramcontent.com/pod-product-compliance
Lightning Source LLC
Chambersburg PA
CBHW040842180526
45159CB00001B/290